CREATIVITY- THE ROAD TO SURVIVAL IN FUTURE OF WORK

THE UNSTOPPABLE CREATIVE

REEMA NAKRA

BlueRose Publishers

First Published in May 2021

ISBN: 978-93-5427-892-1

BLUEROSE PUBLISHERS

www.bluerosepublishers.com

info@bluerosepublishers.com

+91 8882 898 898

Cover Design:

Nirmal K Manoj

Typographic Design:

Vaishnavi Tiwari

Distributed by: BlueRose, Amazon, Flipkart

Look for the unexpected, step out of your own experience!

THINK!

Reema Nakra

Foreword by Pankaj Dubey

Having worked in the corporate world for over two decades, I must say that I agree completely with the essence of the book. Creativity is the only solution for the growth of individuals as well as any company. Reema has very effectively summarised the difference between the ordinary and the extra-ordinary. It is the extra that you deliver over your competitors that differentiates you and your brand and paves your path to success. With the support of technology, companies catch up with innovations very quickly and therefore, the difference in your product or service would not be too substantial, nor would it last for an extensive period. Competition will catch up swiftly. But if you value creativity, you can still stay ahead of your competitor. It is creativity and the extra that you deliver, which makes your brand a success.

I am glad that Reema has laid down details of the future of work that elucidates the foundation of success in the corporate world to the readers. This book functionally discusses the use of creativity and how you can use it to your advantage, in order to achieve your own definition of success. Each of its seven chapters concisely and wonderfully highlights with apt examples and accurate information, how innovation has been used in the past, how it is being used currently, and the future of innovation. Every reader has the ability to create something extraordinary, and this book could be a great help or an important step in your journey. I am sure this book will be of immense value to every reader, if they intently go through the content and make connections in their own world, reading up or watching additional content discussing this topic and starting to develop ideas of their own.

Every journey has a considerable number of steps, and this step is pivotal. I wish each reader takes something away from this book, and makes innovative changes in their own environment, big or small. At the end of the day, you are the future of work, so embark on your unique journey and unleash your creativity along the way. Be nothing less than extra-ordinary.

"Learning gives creativity, creativity leads to thinking, thinking provides knowledge, knowledge makes you great"
Abdul Kalam

Preface

We began 2020 with so much hope and enthusiasm, but by end of March, all that began to ebb away. The spread of the Covid-19 pandemic across the world has forced us to put on hold our plans and dreams, and even our lives. It has caused unprecedented disruption everywhere. One of the most affected groups is of workers. Millions of them have lost their jobs during this pandemic. And, a large number of workers are peering through the fog of uncertainty, wondering, "When will things return to normal?"

When I was exploring ideas for a book on the future of the work, I realised that some workers might never see that normal. They might not have a job to go back to ever. The pandemic has accelerated the adoption of advanced technologies, causing major restructuring of the global job landscape.

Even before the arrival of Covid-19, several companies were investing in automation and artificial intelligence technologies, but the pace of adoption had yet to speed up. We all had almost a decade to prepare and adapt to the new job landscape. Now, the future of work is already here, thanks to the pandemic. Almost overnight, workers have been forced to change the way they work. The sword of Damocles hangs over their heads like never before. And, the concept of stable lifetime employment has been interred for good as well.

How do we deal with this crisis? Well, no solution can be found without determining the exact problem. And, according to me, workers will find themselves out of jobs primarily because they lack creative skills. Creativity is the skill of the future of work. While doing my research for this book, I found that it is going to be the most crucial skill for all jobs, across all industries. The future of work is being shaped by various elements discussed in first book Future of Work: The complete Blueprint, where foundation was laid for operating in new normal. Now we are carry forwarding towards the next step and that is only one skill called Creativity!

But how can we succeed if we do not apply creativity to everything!The Future of work is Imagination, Creativity and Strategy! But question is HOW?

Creativity makes you different from Machines! Yes you heard it Right! Creativity is a skill of future!

In Digitized workplace, creativity plays an important role! You require analytical thinking and innovation, learning strategies and creativity, originality and initiative to thrive!

So let's read how we can apply creative collaborations into our work? What is the power of diversity? What does creativity looks like in action? How is technology re-shaping our creative process?

Its time to re-think what we can do in order to survive and thrive in upcoming years where technology and AI will be going to play an utmost important role in companies! How technology is augmenting human creative abilities? Always remember Humans are strategic and machines ate tactical! Work that requires creative thinking, strategy making is harder to automate! The future of work will be more defined by working collectively in a creative manner!

In this book you will get to know creativity is only solution for growth of the companies, how we can think extraordinary to acquire more clients, what is art of selling, how we can optimise our time, How we can create a culture of innovation, How we can encourage teams to think outside the box, How we can attract diverse group of Talent, How we can organize our work and much more! Leaders will have to behave differently and adopt a creative leadership style in the future of work. It is creative leadership that builds a creative workforce, which helps companies become successful entities.

Creativity is often associated with the arts, while jobs are considered banal and repetitive. In the new job landscape, AI technologies and robotic workforce will take over low-skilled, mundane jobs, while the human workforce will have to learn how to harness creative skills. Does this mean the future of work expects workers to become artists? No, the creativity required here is not that of a painter or a sculptor. It is about dreaming up new ideas, finding new ways of doing things, discovering new needs and market opportunities, solving complex problems, and inventing.

The problem is a lack of skills. The solution is creativity and more creativity. So, to remain relevant and thrive in the future of the work, workers will have to update their skills or reskill themselves. They have to become creative thinkers and not be the underlings who do the same thing every day or follow only orders.

"Creativity takes courage"- Henri Matisse

The economy of tomorrow is innovation-driven. Companies will need their creative workforce to introduce solutions and products that can be used by a majority of the populace. Without them, a company will not gain a competitive advantage in the future and may have to file for bankruptcy.

But, is creativity enough? Innovation cannot happen in isolation. It is collaborative creativity that makes an idea a reality. For creative and innovation processes, we will have to work with teams that are diverse in expertise, experience, and backgrounds. Digital tools will facilitate communication between these teams from across the world. And, only a few members of these teams will be employees of a company – the rest of them will be gig-workers, hired to complete one specific task. We can work for multiple companies at the same time, and earn from them while retaining our autonomy.

We all can turn crisis into opportunities. We will fail to do that by waiting for things to become normal. That normal is not coming back. Let's dive into the waters of the future of work and leverage creativity, to make it our fiefdom. In summing up this books is a complete setup of how creativity will dominate the future of you at work! Gone are the days when creativity was seen as what artists and musicians process. Now it's a crucial skill for professionals in all fields!

Contents

"Creativity is contagious pass it on," –Albert Einstein.

Short Notes

Chapter-1: Creativity is the Skill of the Future!

Creativity, the most innate human skill, is the heart of innovation. We will use it to come up with new solutions and make companies competitive in the future. And, it is the skill that is resilient to future automation.

Chapter-2: Inclusion & Diversity!-A Key to Creativity

Workplaces will have to become more inclusive and diverse. More than a homogenous group, it is a diverse group that can sustain innovation and can satisfy the needs of demanding customers.

Chapter-3: Creativity & Innovation- A Key to success

A company's competitiveness will depend on its capacity to not only adopt new technologies but also innovate. We will leverage our creativity and collaborate with other humans, as well as machine, to create products that benefit humankind

Chapter-4: Creative Communication & Collaboration

The collaboration will enable breakthrough innovation. A lone genius might have been successful in the past, but in the future of work, several creative minds will work together, from different corners of the world, to invent the product of tomorrow.

Chapter-5: Digital Creativity

The digital economy era is upon us. To survive in this era, the workforce will have to improve their digital competencies. We will have to use digital channels to engage with hard-to-please customers and then tap into our creative skills to give them what they need.

Chapter-6: Gig Economy-Creatives on duty

Gig-workers such as freelancers, contractors, and consultants who are equipped with creative skills will find a great number of opportunities in the future of work.

Chapter-7: Creative Sales

In the future, too, companies will need a strong sales team. But, they will no longer be required to make cold calls. They will be needed to create new sales strategies and solve the complex problems of customers. Salesmen will use both technology-generated data and their creativity, to impress customers.

Chapter-8:- Middle-aged workforce challenges & solutions

How middle age workforce will foster creativity, unlearn, relearn and adapt to future of work.

Conclusion: Creativity in Future of Work

There will always be work for individuals who are creative.

****

According to Anthony Jay:- "The Uncreative Mind can spot wrong answers but it takes a very creative minds to spot wrong questions"!

You See things; and you say 'why', I dream things that never were; and I say, 'Why not'?

George Bernard Shaw

About Author

Reema Nakra is the founder of Delhi-based Talent Search Management Consulting (TSMC), an HR Consulting company into recruitment services,L&D Services and HR technology solutions. An experienced staffing specialist, she has worked with various corporate houses and businesses, and has recruited for them some of the best talents and trained their leadership teams. She is a perceptive observer and an excellent communicator and has a great appetite for learning. Reema writes books that explore the future of the work, as it will dramatically change the way people work. "Future of Work: The Complete Blueprint" is the title of her first book.

Reema established TSMC in 2019. In a short time, she has built for herself a strong reputation. She is known for her impeccable work ethics, strong relationship building and engagement skills, and a positive attitude. She has done her post-graduation in human resources from the Institute of Management Technology, and she is a Bachelor of Commerce graduate from Delhi University. She explores and unravels the factors how our future economy will built? How Creativity is art and future of work! Rethink what your workforce Can Do! Technology will replace some work, but it doesn't have to replace the people who have done that work. Future of human work is imagination and creativity! Creativity helps you to see a big picture.

Creativity is big motivation-Doing something creative always lifts up your spirit. It can make you more productive .Creative people are always looking for new ways to solve problems, as well, which sparks innovation and increased efficiency. It's a valued skill in any field. Innovative solutions rise from creative thoughts.

Let's witness together the major shift in digital world of new era! The future of works means few hours spent on site or locked in cubicle Or punching a time clock, it means remote teams, separate but collaborative team work, and much more Reema Nakra, has put together in her well-researched book that how trends, changes and workplace adjustments make the future of work creative, flexible, human and possible!

Acknowledgments

I would like to acknowledge with gratitude, the support and love of my family and my parents, they all kept me going and this book would not have been possible without them.

Special thanks to ,

1-Pankaj Dubey, Managing director, Power Global, who helped to make the book a reality

2-Manish Nigam, CEO, Dalmia Healthcare, for sharing your insights and thoughts.

3-Milind Patil- Executive Director, Bharat Petroleum Corporation Ltd,for your wonderful ideas and insights.

4- Dr Kailas Chapatwala, Group President and Global Head,Wind World India Ltd,for excellent insights and wonderful discussion.

5- Anshu shrivasvastva who has read, advice and commented on various chapters, without your support it would not have been possible.

There are many more people I could thank, but time, space, and modesty compel me to stop here.

Sources

Gartner/hbr.org/weforum/bbc/Mackinsey/Cnbc/Engageemployee/Talentinnovation/HBR.com/BBC/Forbes/Eiuperpectives.economist/adobe/nobleprize/solanreview.mit.edu/wired.com/theatlantic.com/hbr.com/Technologyreview.com/deloitte

Future of Work

Chapter-1

Creativity is the Skill of Future

In future of work, creativity still rules! As digital technology is evolving, the work environment is growing, changing and emerging with times! Today's companies are learning to adapt to the creative ways of working with flexible workforce and modern workplace! Companies are trying to establish and create new culture! Many companies have been adopting a flexible approach to work like providing work from home facility, flexible vacations and even getting cubicles swapped for different types of work stations!

We are in the middle of a seismic shift in workplaces. Robots and machines are taking over jobs that until a decade ago promised lifetime employment to the human workforce. In the beginning, they were brought in to do jobs that were considered too dangerous for humans. Now, they have also taken over jobs that are deemed as too easy, banal, and repetitive. And, in a decade from now, no job is going to remain untouched by automation. Robotics and artificial intelligence (AI) will play prominent as well as minor roles in most offices and factories, which will render millions of humans jobless.

Work is an essential part of our lives. We spend our youth learning skills, with the aim to get a job in a company. These are the skills that our seniors have benefitted from, and our peers are hoping to leverage them. But, can we also benefit from the same skills tomorrow? Flash-forward to 2030, a robot, handling the front desk in an organization, is likely to inform a job seeker who is equipped with today's crucial skills, "We don't hire humans" or "Your skills are redundant."

Jobs of the future will use different skills, as advances in AI will create new fields of work and wipe out most of the current job profiles. But there is one skill of today that will not succumb to the onslaught of robotics and AI, and it will continue to remain indomitable, relevant, and useful tomorrow as well. It is creativity. It is one of the most defining features of humans and cannot be replicated by any machine. We are not talking about the skill of a painter here, but about our innate ability to think creatively in order to solve complex problems in an original and relevant way.

In 2016, the World Economic Forum (WEF) underscored that workers would have to "become more creative" to gain an advantage in the new job landscape, which would be formed due to an "avalanche of new products, new technologies, and new ways of working." It predicted that creativity would become the third-most important skill for employees by 2020. The top two skills were complex-problem solving and critical thinking – both are creative processes.

WEF's "The Future of Jobs Report 2018" lists creativity, originality, and initiative among the skills that would be in demand in 2022, as automation technology would perform most of the routine-based, middle-skilled, and white collared jobs, such as assembling, accounting, data entry, telemarketing, financial analysis, material recording, managing factory operation, machinery repair, and truck driving. And, research and advisory company Gartner has forecasted that "the most-valued work will be cognitive in nature" by 2028 and workers would have to tap creativity, critical thinking, and digital skills, to solve complex problems.

Creativity, just like imagination, commonsense, and judgment, will be harder to automate in the future too. AI, even if it gets more advanced, will not gain the ability to think and design creative strategies. For example, a computer can crunch numbers for financial consultants, but it cannot suggest novel strategies to solve their clients' problems or create attractive marketing materials for them. Creativity is also the bedrock of innovation. And AI will never be advanced enough to head an innovation division, innovation researcher Tony McCaffrey writes in an article, titled "There Will Always Be Limits to How Creative a Computer Can Be," published by *Harvard Business Review*.

McCaffrey and Lee Spector developed mathematical proof to show the creative limitations of computers. They discovered that the fastest modern supercomputer could not list all features of an object. Further, they found that it would fail to explore all features of the thing even if it had started working on the problem in the 1950s. McCaffrey says that when one considers the Obscure Features Hypothesis for Innovation – which states that innovative solutions result from noticing a rarely noticed/never-before noticed feature of a problem, and then building a new solution based on that feature – one can see "how AI may never advance enough to take the jobs of Chief Innovation Officers."

Covid-19 has accelerated the adoption of automation technologies. In some labs, robot scientists have started working independently, as human scientists are reducing their time in the lab, to maintain social distance between them and their colleagues. Robots are conducting experiments and helping speed up scientific discoveries. Will these robots replace human scientists in the future? They might replace lab assistants but not scientists. It is because the latter can harness creativity to come up with new solutions. Robots can undertake time-consuming tasks but cannot think creatively or dream up a new invention.

We cannot compete against technology or stop the rise of robots, who are our future colleagues. We have to learn how to coexist with them and collaborate with them – the way human scientists and robot scientists are collaborating in labs. Our creativity will ensure our leadership roles in the future workplace, as even the most advanced machine cannot hold a candle to this innate skill of ours. It will help us thrive in offices and factories, where it will be rare to find a human employee.

Instead of waiting for the next wave of advancements in AI, and for employers to hand out the pink slips, employees need to reskill themselves to remain a valuable asset to the company. It will also help them make a smooth transition from their current jobs, where machines will replace them, to jobs where their creative skills will be much needed. Students will have to focus on subjects that will help them get into creative fields and make them capable of: solving bigger and complex problems, creating new solutions, communicating with others, generating new ideas, and developing digital content and solutions.

Our Economy is in transition phase, with rise of digital platforms as well as technological trends such as virtual reality, which demand most important skill, creativity and content.

So, what skills will people require to thrive in the imagination economy?

Jobs of the future will also require more social and emotional skills as well as critical thinking, creativity and collaboration.

Machines cannot think out of box or cannot come up with new ideas. This means that highly creative people and critical thinkers will be less likely to lose their jobs to automation. In addition, machines have no empathy. They don't know how to express sentiment resulting in need of emotionally intelligent people with strong interpersonal, listening skills, empathy and responsiveness

People have to be mentally flexible in nature to adapt to the constantly changing world and remain on top of the situation. And who display this phenomena of mental flexibility with problem solving abilities will be in high demand in the imagination economy.

According to the World Economic Forum, creativity will be the third-most-important skill for employees by 2020, behind complex problem-solving and critical thinking. In a report, it says, "With the avalanche of new products, new technologies, and new ways of working, workers are going to have to become more creative in order to benefit from these changes."

Now the question comes, how we can make creative culture at work place? Or how leaders can encourage creativity among employees?

Business Leaders along with team members have to focus on design thinking approach! Leaders should encourage employees to take risk despite of fear of failures, its ok to, be creative, even if they fail! They need to give safety net to employees so that they can feel safe and take risk .They should think differently along with leaders to come up with well-designed programs to foster creativity! They should make an environment where creativity should be rewarded and recognized!

Conclusion

The future workplace will be built on two pillars: AI and creativity. There is unlikely to be a technology that would turn us into humanoid robots so that we can retain our current job profiles. We only have the option of equipping ourselves with creativity: the skill that is resilient to future automation. It is going to play a critical role in getting us through the time of turbulence caused by the culling of millions of jobs. It is the skill that will help us stand us in good stead when there is a rise of the robotic workforce.

There's a science and art to being creative. The organizations should state the value of creativity and regularly reinforce it so employees can see that leadership is recognizing and rewarding it.

Creativity helps us to understand the future of work and it is a reminder to organizations, employers and the workforce that digital skills are nothing without creativity to back them up – whether that is being creative with a spreadsheet or with an easel and paintbrush!

It's no stretch to say creativity is the single-most important skill in the world for all business professionals today to master! Our creativity will keep us employed and open doors to new opportunities

****

Henry Ford - A business that make nothing but money is poor business

A lot of different flowers make a bouquet and, when everyone is included, everyone wins.

~Jesse Jackson

Chapter-2

Inclusion & diversity- A Key to Creativity

BIG THINK

As we scan the current workplaces, we notice a striking lack of diversity. It is still male-dominated, more so at the leadership level. Only a handful of women hold senior leadership positions. The gender inequality might further deepen when artificial intelligence (AI) disrupts the work landscape, as most jobs that women currently hold are susceptible to automation and robotic workforce invasion.

Today's women, unlike their predecessors, are working in all types of industries, even in those sectors that until a few years ago only hired men. But, there more visible presence in workplaces does not mean that they hold influential positions or have the power to make crucial decisions. A significant number of women work as farm and construction workers, office assistants, secretaries, cashiers, data entry clerks, and front-desk receptionists. These are all non-creative, repetitive jobs that offer no challenges or an opportunity to solve complex problems. They will be the first to get eliminated when companies adopt automation and AI technologies.

And, the low-skilled women employees are going to be more affected than their male colleagues, during the first wave of automation. A study done by McKinsey Global Institute, titled "The future of women at work: Transitions in the age of automation," predicts that automation will displace 30 per cent of the women workforce globally by 2030, and in India, up to 12 million women could lose their jobs in the same period.

It has not been easy for women to gain entry into workplaces. They had to fight long battles on multiple fronts and overcome tons of obstacles and prejudices, to get welcomed inside edifices where only men had – and continue to have – the power to call the shots. Automation now threatens to usurp their workspaces and halt their advancement, both in the professional sphere and in society. All their successes might come to naught if millions of girls and women fail to become part of the future job landscape. And, it is not only women, but people from lower socio-economic backgrounds and persons with disability are also facing this time of rapid and dramatic workplace changes and job uncertainty.

They might survive the upheavals caused by robots and AI only if they are equipped with the professional-life-saver float called creativity. This human skill is critical to protect workers from automation. But, then, a majority of them have never pursued an education or undergone training that would have enabled them to flourish in creative fields. They do not know how to tap into creative thinking. Therefore, we see that women, people from lower socio-economic backgrounds, and other underprivileged communities, and persons with disabilities continue to be underrepresented in fields where creativity is needed. We cannot expect them to solve complex problems, think of new ideas, and create innovative solutions. And, in the future of work, there is no place for those who cannot invent, think outside the box, or communicate.

But, a homogenous workforce is less likely to provide a company with a competitive advantage or make it more successful. Even in the golden era of AI, companies that are committed to diversity, and encourage inclusive practices, are going to reap the benefits of increasing profits, because when a diverse group works together, it makes the best decisions, generates useful and original ideas, and produces more creative solutions. Homogenous groups, on the other hand, bring nothing new to the table. Their ideas are stale, and they often make bad decisions. They fail to think of alternative courses of action, as all of them have only one way of seeing things due to their similar life experiences and expertise. And, as tech giant Apple says, "New ideas come from diverse ways of seeing things."

It will serve companies well if they make diversity and inclusion a norm in their future workplaces. They are the transformative forces that can turn a company grappling with losses into a thriving entity. And, "diversity + inclusion = better business outcomes," according to research done by Deloitte, a multinational professional services network.

The future of work is inclusive. Diversity in the workplace is not just a valuable asset; it's inevitable.

Firstly, diversity is a valuable asset.

Mckinsey research clearly shows that companies that are more diverse are more productive, more efficient and give better returns to shareholders. This benefit comes from a number of sources. When we celebrate diversity and inclusivity is mainstreamed, we can retain our people. They are happy and perform more. And as we all know happy workers tend to happy investors.

Diverse companies are more creative and agile, we can only have that diversity of perspective from diversity of work force. if you want to reach majority of people who have diverse backgrounds and are looking for different approaches ,your market strategy has to be aligned with same. Secondly, diversity is inevitable. Organizations that do not accept diversity will die out.

The Cost of Getting Diversity Wrong

Source-theGuardian.com

In 2018, two men were sitting, chatting in a Starbucks in Philadelphia. Like many others, they were continuing a conversation long after they had finished their coffee.

Although several others in the store were similarly without drinks, a Starbucks employee called the police to have the two men arrested for trespassing as they refused to buy coffee. The difference is that these two men were black.

The ensuing media storm and boycott forced Starbucks into action. They shut down every store worldwide to conduct mandatory racism training. This is how serious it is to get diversity right the first time.

Culture of business needs to change from the bottom up .Companies should have that goodwill of being an inclusive workplace, then achieving diversity is easy. Companies have to change their recruitment strategies, generally men's are persistently considered more competent and better leaders regardless of objective evidence. This bias influences every part of the hiring process.Organisations should offer job based on competency and actual potential rather than cultural fit. Companies have to change the focus of diversity initiatives .we need a full culture change and evaluation from diversity perspective.

Diversity, equity and inclusion are key elements of success in the digital workplace.

It's important to note that inclusion is different from diversity. You can hire a diverse workforce, but if they don't feel embraced by their colleagues, if they don't feel supported by executive leadership, and if they don't feel empowered to drive change and share their perspectives, they are not included. Creating a culture of inclusion requires that everyone feels included, everyone participates and everyone works together to support the same goals. And while it starts with recruiting and training, it can also be supported with technology. Recruit for a More Diverse Workforce

QI Group Executive Chairman Vijay Eswaran states that both companies and employees benefit from diversity in the workplace. He calls it an "invaluable asset" in an article written for the World Economic Forum (WEF), titled "The business case for diversity in the workplace is now overwhelming."

Unlike companies that have a homogenous workforce, inclusive and diverse workplaces are breeding grounds for innovation as well. Eswaran believes that such workplaces can "foster innovation, creativity, and empathy." These are the key factors that transmute a small entity into a hugely successful, mammoth conglomerate. Qantas CEO Alan Joe, too, advocates for inclusive and diversity at work.

Joe, often called the "aviation turnaround man," once pulled back Australia's flag carrier Qantas from the brink. In 2013, the company was in dire straits and had suffered its first billion-dollar loss – the lowest point in its 99-year-old history. In response, Joe introduced a series of daring measures, to increase Qanta's revenue by 2017. His measures paid off, as the company rebounded from record losses to record profits soon. Qantas profits were up fivefold in less than five years. What helped this company make such a spectacular comeback? Joe said to The Australian that his company had a "very diverse environment and a very inclusive culture," which enabled them to get "through the tough times." It is because of diversity they could generate "better strategy, better risk management, better debates … better outcomes."

The adoption of technologies might improve performance and speed up processes, but it is not going to make companies immune to potential losses. When they go through turbulent times, they will have to seek the help of their best brains, to generate better strategies and solutions. So, in the future too, there will be a great need for diverse ideas and diversity of creative thinking.

The robotic workforce might take over human jobs but they cannot diminish the importance of humans who are customers or end-users, and who do not belong to one stratum of society. They cannot blow into smithereens their demands for new products as well. Customers will continue to remain the king for companies. Center for Talent Innovation's report, "Innovation, Diversity, and Market Growth," says that a diverse workforce, which is inclusive of women and other unprivileged groups, "confers a competitive edge in terms of selling products or services to diverse end-users." It also notes that "diverse individuals are better attuned to the unmet needs of customers or clients like themselves." A new product or solution is created as a result of this. And, for innovation, companies again need a creative and diverse workforce.

Companies need to begin thinking about how they could make their employees more creative. They need to provide new learning opportunities, organise training sessions, conduct workshops so that their current workforce can upgrade their skills and become capable of solving complex problems. They also need to continue hiring new talents without any bias. For this, they can take the help of an AI that can reduce hiring biases and help build a diverse, equitable, and inclusive workplace of the future. And, as Cook says, "We must address the broad underlying challenges, offer new opportunities, and create a future generation of employees as diverse as the world around us."

Conclusion

Companies can use AI technologies to create a diverse and inclusive workforce. Such a group of employees will sustain innovation, expand the business, satisfy a wide variety of customers, and quadruple profits. Everyone benefits. Companies also need to play a proactive role in reducing the gender gap and ensuring that their women workforce does not disappear when robots and AI technologies take over their low-skilled jobs . They must hire more women, train them, and give them leadership roles. And, in return, the creative women will help companies thrive in the innovation economy of tomorrow.

****

Diversity is the mix. Inclusion is making the mix work. ~Andres Tapia

I have no special talent, I am only passionately curious
-Albert Einstein

Chapter-3

Creativity and Innovation- A Way to Success

The image of robots swarming into factories across the world is no longer an imagination of a sci-fi writer but a reality of the future of work. They and other advanced artificial technologies (AI) might not yet conspire to make humans their slaves and become rulers of the Earth, but they will become an integral part of our workplaces. And, we might see them elbowing out an entire generation of workers, especially those who handle repetitive, tedious tasks. There will, however, be a limit to what AI can do in the future of work. We might not see it heading a team of innovators. On the floor where some of the most brilliant minds will collaborate for the germination of an idea, AI will just play the role of a tool. It will be at the beck and call of a creative employee.

Innovation is imperative for the success of businesses. And, tomorrow, it will become even more crucial for them, as their competitiveness will depend on its capacity to not only adopt new technologies but also innovate.

Automation and AI will transform the way companies work. They will enhance and speed up their operations as well as radically increase their efficiency and productivity. But, with almost all companies, in all industries, jumping on the AI bandwagon, there will not be much to differentiate between them – if they have zero to show in their innovation basket. It is the innovation that will give them a distinctive aura, a competitive advantage, and help them become truly successful, and as *Apple* Co-*founder* and IT creative genius late Steve Jobs once said, "Innovation distinguishes between a leader and a follower."

When we think of innovation, our first thought is to create a new technology or solution. But, it is actually much broader in scope. Oxford Learner's Dictionaries defines "innovation" as, "the introduction of new things, ideas, or ways of doing something." So, it encompasses new products as well as a new way of doing things. "Innovation can be manifested in a new product design, a new production process, a new marketing approach, or a new way of conducting training," American Academic Michael E. Porter writes in an article titled "The Competitive Advantage of Nations," published by *Harvard Business Review.*

As per Manish Nigam, CEO, 'Dalmia Healthcare Ltd' Creativity is a habit and attitude of mind, it's a skill with potential to expand an individual's employability exponentially. Innovation and creativity is all about ability to look at things differently, generate new ideas, look for simplifying complex things, be curious to know 'Why?', and 'Why not?' Creativity is foundation for innovation, problem-solving, change-management and adaptability".

The future of work will affect both employees and employers. Creativity and entrepreneurship form a perfect combination. Its a crucial factor to entrepreneurs for overall success. Creative workforce can be a game changer in your company. The major contributor to the growth of economy is business and there is a huge impact of creativity in same. A blend of technology and creativity in the activities of employer is very helpful in strengthening the business .An employer needs to be innovative for beating the competition in the market .Creative people brings productive change in the system. Creativity can lead to the creation of new business lines and improvement of existing businesses. Its crucial tool for strategic decision making.

Now next question is how we can shape employer's creativity. Few of those factors are knowledge, education, cultural background and technologies. The big the knowledge base of person, the more ideas he can achieve which in turn leads to the creation of new and innovative services for products. High level of creativity and innovation are related with high levels of education and optimism. In shaping the business most important skill for employer is creativity.

In Today's world, due to globalization there is international availability of all products that leads to their access of customers very easily. Now big question is what and how companies do in a market already flooded with a product with many choices available for customers and people have their own preferences. How can companies make their product stand out from the rest? All these questions can only be answered only through creative minds. A creative mind is a artist with most unthinkable ideas.

Digitalisation has created a new breed of customers. Traditional channels and old strategies are proving to be ineffective in engaging with them and meeting their shifting needs. And, customers have yet to realize some of their most essential needs. Companies will have to perceive them, as well as the new market opportunities, and dream up viable solutions and strategies. The introduction of a new product that catches the attention of a large group of people – and which is going to be beneficial to the general society – is going to be the main determinant of a company's future success. If they fail to offer new outstanding experiences, they will become like Nokia or Blackberry.

On January 9 of 2007, Steve Jobs introduced the iPhone to the world, saying "revolutionary and magical product that is literally five years ahead of any other mobile phone." And, nearly 1.4 million iPhones were sold by November, and Time Magazine called it the "invention of the year." This product turned the fortune of Apple and made it one of the most valuable companies of the world – in August 2020, it had a market cap of USD 2 trillion. The launch of the iPhone also triggered the downfall of Nokia and Blackberry. It made them obsolescent overnight.

On the day Steve Jobs unveiled iPhone, Nokia was an undisputed market leader in the mobile phone market, while Blackberry was the prized possession of businesses and governments. But, both of them failed to offer new and better features and adapt to new technologies – for example, android; and hence, it did not take them long to go bust. Kodak is another company that came crashing down because it was not quick enough to perceive the demand of tomorrow. Once a camera giant, it had to file for bankruptcy in 2012, as it was late to realise that the digital camera was the "game-changer" and the new need of its potential customers. According to *BBC*, Kodak's demise was because they were "out-innovated in the technology they had pioneered for over a century."

Companies cannot be slow to respond to rapid changes, and in a highly competitive market, they cannot afford to rest on their laurels. For the company that keeps standing on the same spot and selling the same block of achievement, it can precipitate a swift death. It is only innovation that will ensure its profitable existence for decades as well as turn a crisis into opportunities.

Innovation, however, is not an automatic function or something that shows up out of thin air. And, an AI humanoid robot cannot hand over a new product to us if we say, "Quickly, give me an original solution to launch tomorrow." Companies have to invest in knowledge and human skills, along with technological assets. Once it is done, someone has to think outside-of-the-box, come up with good and big ideas, and convert them into most-wanted, successful solutions. For all these, the innate human skill creativity is very much needed.

Companies cannot just spend money on technologies to build a department for R&D, or research and development, overlooking the human that will ultimately make it run. There will be no inventions of the year if a team of humans is not bouncing off ideas or doing creative brainstorming to make spectacular breakthroughs. Steve Jobs said, "Innovation has nothing to do with how many R&D dollars you have. When Apple came up with the Mac, IBM was spending at least 100 times more on R&D. It's not about money. It's about the people you have, how you're led, and how much you get it."

For companies, they have only two choices: either innovate or die. So, in the future of work, they will always need humans for the development of new winning formulas, which will enable them to remain profitable and competitive for years. And, AI can be used as a "catalyst to push our human creativity," Author Bernard Marr writes in an article titled "Can Machines and Artificial Intelligence be Creative," published by *Forbes*. He believes that it is the human and machine collaboration that produces, "exciting results – novel approaches and combinations that likely wouldn't develop if either were working alone." Instead of seeing AI as job takers, we need to see it as a tool that will "augment" our creativity, according to Barr.

We will see the human workforce gradually transitioning to creative jobs, where tons of lucrative opportunities will open. To grab these oppotunities, we will have to expand our knowledge, upgrade our skills, acquire new ways of doing things, continue to explore, and importantly, we will have to learn how to collaborate and communicate. All of these will enhance our creativity and enable us to unleash disruptive innovation.

Conclusion

Creativity and innovation are the keys to successful organisations.The companies with innovative ideas and approach are inclined towards long term success. When we apply creativity and innovation to everything ,we are able to stay ahead of changing marketplace and the competition .Innovation is based on knowledge and coming up with something new, that has never done before. Creativity and innovation are interconnected and are useful during strategic planning's in an organization.. Innovation can't exist without creativity. An organization that focus on creativity and innovation processes is one that has a shining future.

Companies need growth to survive in the future. For this, they have to foster innovation in their workplaces. They, however, cannot expect inventions after firing their human workforce, to make space for AI and robots. Humans are very much needed to build solutions that can effectively solve real-life problems, as they are equipped with creativity. But, innovation cannot happen in isolation. So, in the future of work, we will see creative humans collaborating with other humans as well as with machines, to offer exceptional customer experience.

Duke Ellington- I don't need time, what I need is deadline

Collaboration, Creativity and respect build lifelong connections that matter and make a difference, propelling us to work together across all boundaries

- Diane Luna

Chapter-4

Creative Collaboration & Communication

What type of stories will top bosses tell when talking about leadership, over the next decade? They are most likely to revolve around technologies and how they have helped their organisations become more agile, nimble, competitive, and profitable. Artificial intelligence (AI) might feature as the protagonist in many of these stories. In some corners of the world, we might also see some bosses narrate stories about human ingenuity and creativity, collaborative spirit, passion, compassion, and invention. We need more of these second type of leaders in the future of work.

We are living through a great shift in how we work. Our traditional workplaces are getting flattened and new edifices, built on the foundation of advanced technologies, are coming up. People in high places are reorganising their workforce as well as rethinking their business models and processes. They are also overseeing the human-to-automation transition. And, as they are the commanders and decision-makers and not minions and submitters, it is a common perception that adoption of automation and AI will not hurt those who are in leadership positions. Leaders must not get lulled into complacency, believing this perception. They will have to remain on their toes because no job is safe after the AI revolution.

The initial transition phase might inoculate the chiefs against job loss and irrelevance. But, once this transition is complete, they, too, will have to face the abyss of uncertainty. "There is no reason to believe that leadership will be spared the impact of AI," Tomas Chamorro-Premuzic, Michael Wade, and Jennifer Jordan write in an article titled "As AI Makes More Decisions, the Nature of Leadership Will Change," published by *Harvard Business Review*. The AI "will supplant many aspects of the 'hard' elements of leadership – that is, the parts responsible for the raw cognitive processing of facts and information," according to them.

In the future of work, the role of leaders will fundamentally change. The new job landscape will severely curtail their positional and hieratical powers. There will be no place for the alpha-male type of leaders who wield authority, think they are the sole experts on everything on Earth and beyond, and believe that they are the cleverest and the smartest people in the room. In their article, Chamorro-Premuzic, Wade, and Jordan note that leadership qualities such as "deep domain expertise, decisiveness, authority, and short-term task focus," are losing their importance. Instead, leaders will require soft skills such as "humility, adaptability, vision, and constant engagement." Leaders can no longer be conformists. They will have to behave differently as well as acquire new critical skills, just like those handling low-skilled jobs.

As our economy becomes innovation-driven and advanced technologies make our workspaces more decentralised, leaders of today cannot demonstrate their leadership ability by being cooped up inside their comfort zones. And, their work is not over after opening the doors for smart machines, as the adoption and use of technology offer them no guarantee that they can work in the same position until the day they decide to hang up their boots. To be relevant in the future of work, they will have to craft vivid visions.

They will have to perceive future trends before their competitors do, find new ways of doing things, come up with disruptive strategies that have the potential to make innovation a reality, as well as they should know how to encourage and inspire their co-workers. Also, as global and local competition intensifies, leaders will need the acumen to make bold movies.

However, without creativity, leaders cannot achieve their short-term goals or long-term goals, even if they burn the proverbial midnight oil. They will fail to execute the business vision as well. So, before they try to navigate through the choppy waters of tomorrow, leaders must first learn how to harness creativity. It is the skill of the future of work and crucial for effective leadership.

But, can leaders invent something alone? or Can someone transform into a great leader just by holding the wand of creativity? The answer to both these questions is a BIG NO. Without a team, even the most creative leader will have nothing to show for his/her time behind the desk. "One of the greatest lessons of leadership is that the best leaders don't work alone," Forbes Councils Member David Dewolf writes in an article for *Forbes*, titled "The Best Leaders Don't Work Alone: How Leading With Trust Builds Great Teams." What makes leaders "great" is their ability to "put together great teams." Such teams enable world-class discoveries and develop solutions that can make the life of humans better. American author Seth Godin says, "leadership is the art of giving people a platform for spreading ideas that work."

In the future of work, a person in a leadership position will need these six factors to make a breakthrough and achieve success for the company: solo creativity, the creativity of team members, diversity, collaboration, communication, and reskilling platforms.

Leaders will have to treat their team members as "thought partners," and understand their vision and perspectives, as well as solicit their critical views, suggestions and regular feedback. They have to move from "we will do things this way" and "This is what I think" to "What do you think?" and "Why?" or "Let's hear what he/she has to say." And, they should not shy away from becoming the chief reskilling officer of the team.

The new job landscape requires new skill sets. Some team members might not have them. Instead of complaining, grumbling, and signing on the employment termination letters, leaders will have to encourage their team members to update their skills or reskill themselves. Not only encourage but also teach them how to leverage their critical thinking and creative skills. Great leaders are not only creative themselves but they also create opportunities for others to be creative. This helps build a team that is highly creative at work – which makes the company competitive in the future.

American Cardiologist Mark Fishman, also former president of the Novartis Institutes for BioMedical Research (NIBR), has three set of advice for leaders who are working in a creative environment. Teresa Amabile and Mukti Kaire quoted him as saying in an article titled "Creativity and the Role of the Leader," published by *Harvard Business Review*, "Know where you are in the game. Appreciate the different creative types among your people -- and realize that some are better at certain phases than others. And be very tolerant of the subversive."

Leaders will have to be prepared for the future of work, and therefore, they need to now embrace a more creative leadership style.

Late Stefan Hawking, one of the most brilliant theoretical physicists in history, had once warned that artificial technology (AI) would replace humans altogether, one day. He called it a "new form of life" that has the potential to outperform us. Hawking was talking in general and not particularly about our future workplaces. But, at present, it seems like a correct prophecy made for the job landscape, which is on the cusp of dramatic transformation that will see robots take over vast swathes of workplaces that employ a great number of humans. How do we fight back and not cede all our job territories to the rapidly advancing AI technologies? We will have to leverage the 3Cs – collaboration, communication, and creativity. They are the weapons that will empower us and ensure that we do not become subservient to robots.

Automation will wipe out several jobs but it will also create not-yet-thought-of opportunities, especially in industries where innovation is – or becomes – the driving force. If we have the skill of creativity and can invent, we can avert our slide into irrelevance, as robots cannot occupy positions that have to deliver new ideas, original and critical solutions, and think of disruptive innovation. They might have phenomenal accuracy and unlimited memory but are bereft of imagination and creativity.

But, is creativity enough? Can we become irreplaceable in the future of work just by holding this one ace card? No, it is not enough. We will have to hold all the aces, including collaboration, communication, and a growth mindset. Without them, our creativity might not do wonders for our careers. But, when we work with people of different skills and mindsets and from diverse backgrounds, we can build extraordinary solutions and become valuable assets for our companies.

Let's talk about how we can collaborate at work for the furure.We have many forms for same like Meetings- An opportunity for discussions and collaborations. Quick Q'S is another thing that helps to get collaborative, you can frame different questions for your team to have their opinions on specific projects and thereby can take a collective call on same. Brainstorming sessions is also a great way to coming up collectively and sharing better ideas for solving a problem. Also online chats, video calls, screen shares that allow our teams to see exactly what is there on other side. Collaborations has never been this easy.

For long, there has been a myth that innovation happens, or scientific discovery is made, when a genius works in isolation, in a closed room. Sir Isaac Newton, the man who discovered gravity, was one of the biggest proponents of isolated working. The title of "solitary genius" suited him, as his creativity flourished once he shut the door on people and distractions. But, Nobel laureate in Chemistry Martin Chalfie, on the other hand, had initially quit his scientific career because of the myth of the lone genius. He told The Nobel Prize website that his first experience with science "ended badly" because he thought he would have to do experiments alone and make breakthroughs without the help of others.

At the time, Chalfie felt that "asking for help was a sign that I was not intelligent enough." He now feels that it was a "destructive attitude." In 2008, Nobel Prize was awarded jointly to him Osamu Shimomura and Roger Y. Tsien for "the discovery and development of the green fluorescent protein, GFP." Their collaboration enabled them to make this major scientific discovery. The examples of breakthroughs due to joint efforts are in plenty, including that of the special theory of relativity. Albert Einstein could comprehend this theory only after a lot of discussions with his old classmate Michele Besso.

Innovation Biome author Kumar Mehta writes in Forbes, "Innovation in isolation is hard because human creativity needs idea sharing and interaction to flourish." According to him, a lone inventor working "alone in a dusky lab," cannot make breakthroughs. Inventors "thrive when ideas are shared, challenged, and refined." Salesforce President Gavin Patterson, too, shares the same views. He writes in an article for the World Economic Forum (WEF) that most real innovations happen because of working together and not because of individuals working in isolation. He believes that when experts in different fields have collaborated to achieve a common goal, it has resulted in the biggest successes.

We also become highly effective and efficient and achieve a high level of creative productivity because of collaboration. It is because we learn from others new ways to solve complex problems, can identify the minutest glitch, and overcome unexpected bottlenecks easily, as well as we can share the workload, resources, and knowledge. Also, we gain the freedom to think more radically and creatively. These things help in developing a great solution within the stipulated time.

A high level of cooperation, however, can be achieved only through communication. It is critical for a fruitful collaboration because, to create a new solution, we will have to interact with highly educated specialists, experts from different fields, and a diverse group of team members, who might not be located in the same office or in the same time zone. And, we might have to work with them in the virtual sphere.

Unlike the last century, it is no longer difficult to communicate and collaborate even if members of our team members are in different corners of the world. There are advanced tools and platforms available, to facilitate our interaction with others. They allow us to brainstorm and solve issues together, develop consensus, and bring all the groups on the same page. And, they help us to bring our creative ideas to life. Microsoft Teams, Slack, Figma, and Adobe Creative Cloud are examples of collaboration and communication platforms. And, according to Unit 9 Head of Design Karol Goreczny, virtual reality and augmented reality will play a "big role" in the creative collaboration process.

In Adobe's "The Future of Creative Collaboration," report, he notes that these great technologies can "bring people together in one virtual room in order to review, provide feedback, while in context to iterate on the actual project." In the same report, Jan Bancroft, associate creative directive at VCCP, says, "AI will help streamline the process and smooth out any lumps." He believes that technology will enable us to "build relationships between teams and disciplines," as well as offer "options and opportunities to get the best out of an idea."

AI technology is not going to interfere with our creativity. It is going to help us generate better ideas by enabling collaboration and communication with others. Because of that, we will deliver results fast and create better solutions.

Collaboration, however, will not benefit everyone. Those who are not creative enough, do not have specialised skills, cannot dream up new ideas, or are not nimble are less likely to be part of the innovation-centric companies. We have to become experts and arm ourselves with high-level skills, to get an entry ticket to these companies. Companies, on other hand, will have to make employees familiar with the new changes, encourage teamwork, equip them with the new technology tools and give them the training to use them.

We have to adapt and evolve, keeping in mind the jobs that will be available only for humans.

Conclusion

As John Donne a famous writer and poet said once "No man is an island, every man is a piece of continent,a part of main".He expressed the need of us human to be a part of larger community to thrive. This also relates to work place, where we need to cooperate, collaborate and co-create to achieve business objectives.

Creativity is a collaborative act. In digitized workplace the creative collaborators rules. But creativity alone is not enough, success can be achieved by fair communication, collective vision, sharing ideas and working together in creative collaboration. We cannot create something new if see it as a one-person pursuit. Therefore, if we want to remain relevant and not become obsolete in the future, we have to stop working in silos, begin communicating with different groups of people, and be open to the ideas and opinions of others. If we refuse to adapt to the rules of the new work culture, another human will replace us – if not the machine. Collaboration and communication, on the other hand, will allow us to create solutions and products that can be used by a majority. This will help us dominate robotic workforce for decades.

Good leadership is crucial for a company's success. In the future of work, leaders will play a pivotal role. But, they will have to shun their old leadership style and be more creative. They will have to encourage the sharing of ideas, suggestions, feedback, and critical views. In short, they need to learn the art of collaboration and communication. Leaders cannot find a new way of doing or solve a problem by working alone in their office cabins. As many employees might not have creative skills, leaders will have to become their teachers and provide them the platforms to reskill themselves. It is said that creative leadership builds the creative workforce. And, it is this workforce that dreams up and executes an idea, which gives a company its competitive advantage.

****

A successful team is a group of many hands and one mind- Bill Bethel

Everything should be made as simple as possible but not simpler

-Albert Einstein

Chapter-5

Digital Creativity

When future economic historians would discuss the twentieth-century world economy, they would divide it into eras, before and after Covid-19. The coronavirus pandemic has fast-tracked the rise of the digital economy while wrecking the old business systems before time. Even after the pandemic is over, we are not going back to how things were before March 2020. New workplace rules have already been written, keeping in mind the needs and demands of the new digital economy era. We have to quickly adapt to sudden and unprecedented changes in the job landscape, to avoid becoming part of the unemployment statistics. Future of work is transforming by emerging technologies .Digital Technology has started to move from innovation part of process to application of creativity .The more creative job is, less likely to be replaced by job. Digitalization will bring more time for creative tasks with the help of Artificial Intelligence.

With the expansion of digital technology, there has been tremendous increase in number of ways how people can express their creativity. Our new norm for self-expression now a days consist of Artificial intelligence, Podcast, you tube videos, social media and virtual reality. If we look at history, creativity is something to be nourished and cherished and it thrives because of culture and technology.

In the beginning of 2020, we were congregating around water coolers in offices and speaking in jest about the future of work. But, by the end of March, there was a deadly silence in offices all across the world. Employees were cooped up in their houses, as offices, factories, and all other workplaces were shut due to complete lockdown. Those who work in traditional sectors had no other choice but to twiddle their thumbs. They also faced salary cuts and layoffs. The lockdown also affected those who work in technology-centric, non-traditional sectors, but not to a great extent. These employees could maintain their relevancy as they could work from home, using digital tools.

Before Covid-19 upended the world, the global economy was already undergoing digital transformation at breakneck speed. The internet, mobile technology, the internet of things (IoT), and artificial intelligence (AI) were causing the collapse of our old business models, reshaping our traditional workplaces, and facilitating inventions. But, we were not yet completely reliant on digital channels. Such a day was still some time away. The pandemic, however, has made digital central to all our interactions and collaborations. Overnight, it has become critical for our survival. Digitalization is development which gives entrepreneurs enormous opportunities.

McKinsey's report, titled "Digital strategy in a time of crisis," states that the Covid-19 crisis has provided a glimpse into the future world. In this new world, "digital channels become the primary (and, in some cases, sole) customer-engagement model," and automated processes turn into "primary driver of productivity – and the basis of flexible, transparent, and stable supply chains."

The rise of the digital economy was inevitable. Companies had read the tea leaves, and therefore, they were slowly scaling up their digital operations and increasing investments in digital technologies. In 2017, a total of $1.3 trillion was spent globally on digital transformational technologies, including services, hardware, and software, according to tech research company

IDC. At the time, it had predicted that by 2021, this spending would be more than $2.1 trillion. This investment might redouble in certain sectors while in some, such as hotels and air transport, there might be a decline due to the impact of Covid-19. But, it is certain that everyone will have to accept the digital-first way of working.

We will now see companies investing in integrated cloud, automation, AI, advanced data and analytics, and blockchain at an unprecedented speed. But, can businesses survive only by investing in digital technologies? What happens to humans? In the digital era, those who can access technology and digital tools and use them to innovate will remain valuable. That is, the human workforce has not yet become replaceable. We might not be able to congregate around water coolers in large numbers, but we will not lose our leadership positions and the right to dream up new solutions while sipping hot coffee. Technology might hit the headlines more often, but stories of human achievements will continue to be the most sought after. And, our creativity will save us from becoming obsolete. It is because customers will continue to be the King in the digital economy era as well.

Businesses have been forced to adopt digital technologies due to the evolving behaviour of customers, and their new needs. For example, during the lockdown, several retailers digitalised their businesses, as their customers, facing mobility restrictions, were looking for online options. And, a machine or an AI technology did not create the online setup. At a retailer office, a group of humans tapped into their creative thinking to identify the new buying behaviour, determine what exactly customers need, solve complex problems, and develop new sales channels and payment systems. And, they used their ingenuity to design a unique platform that is accessible and user-friendly. Technology only played a supportive role while humans did all the creative heavy lifting.

Digital tools have allowed companies to better engage with all their stakeholders and changed the game of customer interaction. But, they can neither determine the needs of the fickle and hard-to-please customers nor think of an idea that will provide them outstanding experiences. Even the most advanced digital technology cannot change the fortune of a struggling company if it does not know how to connect with its customers, give them what they urgently need, and keep them satisfied. Only humans have the capability to make it an unbeatable entity, as we are imaginative, can think critically, and we can use creativity as a lever. They enable us to come up with solutions to improve customer experience, which is at the heart of the digital economy.

Technology is not the protagonist of digital transformation. It has just empowered it, according to digital analyst Brian Solis, who is also a business strategist and futurist. "Without an end in mind, digital transformation continually seeks out how to use technology in ways that improve customer experiences and relationships," he writes in an article, titled "Digital Darwinism: How Disruptive Technology Is Changing Business for Good," published by Wired.com. Solis says that it is also about the endeavor that develops new business models as well as that creates a way for businesses to stay relevant in a time when customers are becoming increasingly digital.

AI and digital technologies will not hold the reins of the digital economy. They will be in the hands of those who are in leadership positions. They are the ones who will turn technologies into a truly transformative force, and for this, they will leverage their creative skills. And, for success in the digital economy era, businesses will have to introduce new products and solutions, and without human creativity, they will invent nothing. So, businesses have to invest in employees also, and not just digital tools. They have to build their digital competencies.

Becky Frankiewicz and Tomas Chamorro-Premuzic believe that digital transformation is more about talent and less about technology. We can invest in any technology, but our "ability to adapt to an even more digital future depends on developing the next generation of skills, closing the gap between talent supply and demand, and future-proofing your own and others' potential," they write in an article, titled "Digital Transformation Is About Talent, Not Technology," published by Harvard Business.

Becky Frankiewicz and Tomas Chamorro-Premuzic are confident that it is the "focus on the reskilling and upskilling [of] people" that is the strongest bet on the future, which is highly uncertain. They have to be "better equipped to adjust to change."

Conclusion

The pandemic has robbed us of the time that we had, to gain digital competencies. Now that the digital economy era is upon us, and digital transformation is no longer optional, we will have to quickly reskill ourselves so that we can adjust to the new workplace realities. Companies will have to significantly invest in new digital tools, but not at the expense of their employees. It is the innovation that will fuel their growth in the digital economy era, and without creativity, there can be no new product development. So, they should consider giving employees responsibilities that need the pairing of creative skills with technology. This will make companies stand out among their competitors.

Be the change you wish to see in the world-Mahatma Gandhi

The Gig economy is empowerment, this new business paradigm empowers individuals to better shape their own destiny and leverage their existing assets to their benefits

-John Macfee

Chapter-6

Gig Economy-Creative on duties

A generation ago, it was common for a person to have a long career in one company. Most workers entered an organisation in their twenties and only exited it on their retirement day, in their sixties. Millennials moved away from this traditional work arrangement. Unlike their parents, they were not looking for job stability or longevity but flexibility and freedom. They readily forgo the regular monthly income, long-term financial security, and social safety nets, and became free agents. They willingly embraced temporary work engagements. And, their full plunge into the gig economy suddenly expanded a smallish ecosystem of gig workers.

Gig workers existed even before millennials came of age in the mid-2000s. But, they were a fringe community, who often confused others with their job description. If we were to ask veteran gig workers what was the common refrain that they heard at the turn of the century or before that, they would most likely say, it was "Oh freelancer, but what do you actually do?" Today, they might be hearing that only once in a blue moon. With millennials joining the ecosystem, there was a significant increase in the number of gig workers. Soon, their temporary work arrangements were no longer an alien concept, or of lesser dignity than traditional employment, for a lot of people, if not a majority.

The gig ecosystem began buzzing at the start of 2010s, coinciding with the rise of the digital economy. Many choose to work as independent workers, sellers, and contractors, as well as delivery drivers, freelance writers, software developers, designers, videographers, and part-timers; instead of looking for 9-to-5 permanent jobs. In an article for *Reuters*, published in January of 2011, former-Freelancers Union Executive Director Sarah Horowitz, called this *transition* – from traditional employment to *the gig economy* – "*nothing* less than a revolution."

In 1995, Horowitz founded Freelancers Union, a U.S.-based non-profit organisation that provides advocacy, programming, and curated insurance benefits for freelancers. There were not many who understood the term "freelancer" in the mid-90s. And, almost fifteen years later, she noted in her article that the workforce shift to the gig economy was as "significant" as the "transitioned from an agricultural to an industrial economy."

A report by ADP Research Institute, released in February of 2020, noted that the share of gig workers in American businesses increased 15 per cent since 2010. The incredible growth of the gig economy is not just limited to the U.S., but it is a rapidly growing global phenomenon. Today, gig or contingent workers make up about 15-25 per cent of the global workforce, according to Gartner's report. It predicts that they would account for 35-40 percent of the workforce by 2025.

Earlier, companies outsourced some work to independent workers and freelancers, to get it done at a cheaper cost. The cost of enlisting their help for a limited period was less compared to employing permanent employees, who they had to pay not only monthly salaries but also offer other corporate benefits. The 2010s saw the emergence of multinational tech companies whose growth was fueled by independent workers. Without roping in these free agents, these companies could have neither existed nor have enjoyed the fruits of profits. For them, gig workers were a legitimate and important workforce, but they had no full-time employment to offer them. Instead, they provided them with a high level of autonomy and opened doors to earn money by the task, sales, or assignment. Ride-hailing giants Uber and Ola; Airbnb, a vacation rental online marketplace; and e-commerce giant eBay are the pioneers of the gig economy.

Uber and Ola operate a ride-hailing company but own no fleet of cars. They need the labour and cars of drivers – Uber calls them independent contractors – to make their companies run. Similarly, Airbnb rents no asset of its own but it encourages others to share theirs with complete strangers. So, if no renters are willing to host guests or bohemian travelers in their homes, this company will collapse – it almost did because of the coronavirus pandemic crisis. eBay offers tons of products but neither procures nor manufactures any of them. It is a platform that facilities the selling of goods by independent sellers. These and other companies have helped create a larger and diverse pool of gig workers and made their work a viable and culturally accepted career. They have also caused a considerable change to the gig economy, making it more of a digital gig economy or what *the New Yorker* calls, "on-demand, peer, or platform economy."

The current gig economy is internet-enabled. It could not have swelled if there was no spread of high-speed internet connections, across the world, or if smartphones had not become ubiquitous. Digital tools, too, have played a pivotal role in its stunning rise. They have erased geographical boundaries, which have opened floodgates of opportunities for independent workers. In 2016, a report by McKinsey Global Institute, "Independent Work: Choice, Necessity, And the Gig Economy," noted that the independent work was rapidly evolving as "digital platforms create large-scale, efficient marketplaces where workers connect with buyers of services."

In the future of work, the gig economy is where we will find maximum opportunities. As automation and AI technology will lord over low-skilled workers and ultimately, take over their jobs, companies will not need full-time employees to run their operations. They will engage with those who have a specific skillset and can accomplish a specific task. And, this engagement will be for short-term, project-based work. Workers will have the freedom to explore more options and earn money from them.

There is going to be a high demand for creative gig workers. As tomorrow's economy will be innovation-driven, more and more companies, across all industries, will seek talented workers who can harness their creative skills, to dream up ideas that have the potential to become the next disruptive solutions. They are likely to form a virtual team of independent specialists, assign each member a specific task, and support collaboration, to solve a not-yet-noted problem. And the advances in digital technologies enable companies to select the best creative talent for each task, from anywhere in the world. In the gig economy, according to Forbes Councils Member Mike Volkin, "instead of having access to talent in your geographic area, companies can now access highly specialised talent anywhere in the world."

Unlike the traditional workforce, gig workers will be sure-footed when they step into the future of work. There is no job to lose for those who are part of the sharing gig economy, for example, renters at Airbnb. They cannot be given a pink slip or forcibly evicted, as they are the owners of their assets. But, technology might make some of the platform gig jobs redundant. For example, the introduction of driverless taxis in the future might kill the ride-hailing services. And drivers will have to learn new skills to survive.

If creative gig workers keep their skills and knowledge up-to-date, they are expected to become the most-sought-after dazzling stars of the gig economy. And all independent workers have to equip themselves with skills that will be needed tomorrow, even those in creative fields. As the job and tech landscapes are constantly changing, they have to regularly determine, "what kind of expertise I need tomorrow" and "which industry will need what type of skills." Once the answers have been found to these questions, they have to upgrade their skills as quickly as possible so that they can stay ahead of the curve. How can one do that? Well, Volkin says, "The internet has not only given us the power to find opportunities, but also the power to find and get training that is desirable for employers."

Conclusion

Most people become independent workers by choice rather than necessity. It is because the gig economy offers them flexibility and freedom, and they also get to choose assignments that are in sync with their true interests. Unlike the past, people now have more opportunities for freelancer work, and it is because of the new digital platforms. They have made it easy for independent workers to find customers, contracts, and assignments. And, everyone can work in the gig economy if they have internet. But, we have to prepare for the future of work when the set of skills needed to thrive in the gig economy will change. Our creative skills will enable us to keep moving forward even when the traditional job landscape begins to crumble. But, to continue getting gigs in future of work, we have to make our skills and knowledge current.

If People like you, they will listen to you, but if they trust you, they will do business with you

-Zig Ziglar

Chapter-7

Creative Sales

Today, it might be hard to imagine a robot wining the best salesperson of the year award. But, there is every possibility of it happening tomorrow. We can no longer dismiss it as a far-fetched notion of someone with a fertile imagination. Artificial intelligence (AI) has already started making inroads into the sales territory. And, it is only a matter of time before companies across the world raise full battalions of AI-powered sales force.

We are on the cusp of the fourth industrial revolution. It will usher in sweeping changes in industries all over the world. German Economist Klaus Schwab, who is best known as the founder and executive chairman of the World Economic Forum (WEF) wrote in an article for *WEF*, titled "The Fourth Industrial Revolution: what it means, how to respond," the fourth revolution is distinctive from the earlier ones in its "scale, scope, and complexity." He predicted that the transformation caused by it would "be unlike anything humankind has experienced before."

Increased levels of automation and convergence of digital, physical, and biological technologies are driving this new revolution. And, companies, if they do not want to join a group of has-beens, will have to adapt to new ways of working. They will have to embrace new technologies and be the vanguard of change, to remain competitive and profitable. With AI becoming omniscient and omnipresent, many of us might have to board a train called uncertainty, which would take us to a jobless future.

And, as automation and innovation are central to the future of work, we will see many job titles and designations getting consigned to History. The sales and marketing team, however, might survive this dramatic transition. In the future too, companies will have to sell their products and services.

Even the most innovative goods need markets or buyers, and if there are none for them, they become an albatross around the necks of companies. So, the sales team will most likely continue to enjoy their valuable status in a company. But, not every salesperson will be seen as indispensable.

According to M S Patke, Executive Director, Biofuels, Bharat Petroleum Corporation Limited. Strategic Business Units" as a concept is good to create vertically aligned organisations within an Umbrella outfit. Our company had restructured the organisation on these lines and we did achieve the desired results in terms of greater customer focus within each SBU. However we encountered a challenge while we were faced with customer centric issues at granular level. We realised that the ultimate customer for all SBUs is common and hence Project "BPCL first" was launched. This was an inward looking project designed to create a culture of "customer centricity" across the organisation. I had the honour of leading this project as we created Customer Innovation councils across 64 cities (later increased to 100) which were seeing higher growth of petroleum products. All the front line officers were part of this council and they came together to make their common business plan, the ultimate goal being "customer delight". This creative project on "Customer Centricity" saw coming together of all business units to address all the needs of a retail customer and similarly that of an institutional customer. The success was measured in terms of greater customer satisfaction levels as well as new accounts each business unit obtained. This move paved the way for a digitally activated customer care solution as well social media strategy. The future road map included "business analytics" as we weaved an ecosystem around the traditional oil & gas business.

The digital era has changed the game of selling. Traditional sales techniques such as cold calls, bombarding everyone with the same promotional messages, telling customers what they need and why they must buy, and other seller-centric methods are now considered passé. Companies, therefore, do not need a bloated team of front-line sellers. Sales is a big transformation in coming years.It is going through a big revolution,the web is making sales professional more important then ever. Companies are hiring more skill people these days .Now Sales People have to induce creativity in sales pitching.

After years of talking about a customer-centric approach to sales, companies have finally made users the focal point of their sales strategies. This shift has happened primarily due to digitalisation, which has bestowed on customers the self-service capabilities. They can do a lot of product research on their own, and then do the trial, and purchase. And, they no longer want to be told what they need and why. Creative sales professionals have to be problem solver and should continuously brainstorm ways to delight customers. It will be very much need for sales people to keep note of current affairs and monitor events or development that are very much relevant to customers. Sales professional now requires out of box thinking.

In recent years, the behaviour of customers has changed. Social media platforms, referrals by peer groups and influencers, and online reviews and discussions are influencing their purchase decisions, and there is also a marked decline in customer loyalty. Also, smartphones and cheaper data plans have made it easier for them to find out about the range and types of products available in a particular category, and their pros and cons. Equipped with information and many choices, customers have become smarter, more demanding, and harder to please. And, to impress their potential customer-base, companies are increasingly leveraging digital and AI technologies. "AI has the potential to significantly improve businesses' sales and marketing efforts, and thus their fortunes overall," according to a research report by *Harvard Business Review Analytic Services*, titled "Artificial Intelligence and the Future of Sales and Marketing. This Microsoft-sponsored report also underscores that companies might find it difficult to move forward without adopting AI. Their "future competitiveness" depends on it.

The report notes that companies are using AI to identify sales prospects and gain insights into prospects and customers. Consider the example of a southeastern Europe-based mobile gaming company, which is using AI to covert its free-version users to paid customers. The company's executive producer said to *Harvard Business Review* that they turn their leads into paying users through a three-step process.

First, they identify prospects, "the high-value players," on social media platforms. They target them based on a variety of data and behaviour, which indicates that these players are "most likely to stay in the game and convert to a paid membership." Then, the company taps into its own algorithms and in-house platform, to analyse the in-game behaviour of the free-version using gamers. Those who are more likely to stay – the real gaming enthusiasts – are encouraged to upgrade to the paid version. Finally, the company "uses AI to predict churn – who is likely to leave the game – and intervene with special offers," according to the report.

MIT Technology Review Insights survey report, titled "*How AI is changing the customer experience,*" too, notes that AI is quickly changing the way companies engage with their customers. Its survey of 1,004 business leaders found that after customer service, the sales and marketing department was where they were using AI effectively.

Millions of jobs in sales are expected to vanish entirely because of AI. Will it really cause the death of the salesman? We might see a great number of salespeople off the road, no longer traversing known and unknown places, to meet their sales targets. But, this does not mean we will have to write an elegy for all of them. AI will make only some salespeople's jobs irrelevant, according to Forbes Councils member Matthew Cook, also founder and CEO of SalesHub. They are the jobs that do not contribute to the company's revenue, such as "prospecting and qualifying leads, scheduling meetings, sending follow-up emails, and building reports." AI will handle these time-consuming, repetitive, and mundane jobs in the future of work. Salespeople, on the other hand, will have to focus on "building relationships and solving client problems with creative solutions."

AI generated data is already enabling companies to find leads, gain predictive insights, determine the persona of their potential customers, and what they value and dislike.

But, a sales process hinging solely on data will not give the desired result or increase revenue. Data-based sales will have to involve creativity, as well.

To create a winning sales strategy, companies will have to strike a balance between data and creativity. Together, they will drive growth for companies in the future. And, salespeople who are capable of doing bold creative thinking will set themselves up for success. It is because customers are not a monolithic group. Each one is unique and has a set of distinctive needs. And, data provides information about what matters the most to consumers but it offers no suggestions on how to engage with each one of them and solve each of their needs. Like today, tomorrow also, it is the salespeople who will have to step up to interact with customers and come with sales strategies that are born of creative thinking.

Node Founder and CEO Falon Fatemi believes that the most effective salespeople "leverage their creativity to gain a leg up on competitors." And, customers acknowledge those salespeople who are "creative problem solvers," she writes in an article for *Forbes*, titled "Why Creativity is a Secret Weapon in Sales?" It is because they try to understand how a product or a service is "uniquely positioned to help each customer achieve his/her business outcomes."

Both salespeople and companies will have to change their mindsets and redesign their sales processes, keeping in mind the AI invasion and needs of customers. Companies, in particular, will have to identify the core sales skills that their sellers will need in the future and then sponsor their reskilling education.

The future of work demands that salespeople gain a broader knowledge of their field of work and arm themselves with creativity and critical thinking. Leveraging them, they can interpret the data accurately, understand the value of each data point, create a result-oriented sales strategy, engage with customers in a meaningful way, handle trickiest situation, and monetize their sales process.

Also, because of their quick and creative thinking, they will have the ability to stop a robot sales representative from committing a big blunder in the future.

Conclusion

AI is going to significantly disrupt what salespeople do. In the future of work, a lot of their current sales activities will get automated. Moreover, customers are no longer dependent on them to make their purchase decisions. Social media platforms and search engines have enabled them to look for information, compare products and prices themselves. But, automation does not mean salespeople will become an extinct workforce. They will continue to remain crucial for their companies. Companies that foster creativity are more likely to perform better in terms of revenue growth. With creativity being key skill investment pays big returns in form of sales excellence and results. Creative sales is new way of selling .It requires great persistence, preparation and sales strategy. They, however, will have to learn new skills to understand and interpret data, as well as know how to work with AI, and become complex problem solvers – not just remain sellers.

The only source of knowledge is experience
-Albert Einstein

Chapter-8

Future of Work: Middle-Aged workers challenges & solutions

Older age a competitive disadvantage or advantage?

How does our post-Covid-19 world of work look like? The pandemic has unleashed changes that were expected to take place by 2030. It has fast-forwarded the "future of work" by a good decade. In 2020, the lockdown across the world forced us to work from our bedrooms, dining tables, and couches. And in our absence from our workplaces, automation, digitalisation, and advances in artificial intelligence (AI) unfurled their flags of disruption; permanently altering the job landscape across the world. A lot of mundane, repetitive jobs have vanished while we were locked inside our houses. It has rendered millions of people jobless. Furthermore, there has been a shift in the kind of skills that companies now require.

The rise of the technology-driven world of work has created an unprecedented situation. There is a genuine fear that millions of workers would become obsolete once advanced technologies are done reshaping our workplaces – built around creative humans and intelligent machines. And middle-aged workers are expected to suffer maximum job losses because of widespread automation and adoption of AI and other advanced technologies. Those who do repetitive jobs and have a lower level of skills will certainly become part of the technological unemployment story. How do these workers move out of the vulnerable group and become "perfect candidates" for companies? Well, they have only one option to pick – upgrade their skill sets significantly.

A large share of jobs will disappear in the future of work. But this does not mean that the world is going to run out of work. The avalanche of AI and automation will create new jobs too, not just inter the old ones. But these jobs are going to be different and will demand different skill sets. Middle-aged workers will have to accept the new reality and equip themselves with new skills; otherwise, they will have to live in a world without work. A *McKinsey*'s report, titled "Jobs lost, jobs gained: What the future of work will mean for jobs, skills, and wages," notes that the human workforce will spend more time on activities that machines cannot handle and less time on "predictable physical activities and on collecting and processing data" that machines can perform. To remain relevant and competitive in the new world of work, workers will have to acquire "social and emotional skill and more advanced cognitive capabilities, such as logical reasoning and creativity."

As Dr Kailas Chapatwala,Group President and Global Head,Wind World India Ltd, has rightly said-"Middle age workforce is highly valued as they bring years of knowledge, skill and experience. These workers are often able to provide leadership and mentoring to younger generations. Companies needs to reskill and up skill their employees, as technology advances and the market changes, the pressure grows on older workers to keep skills up to date through training, on the job learning, mentoring and job rotation. Training and up skilling older workers is crucial for the growth and development of the companies. Older employees can be trained in the creative process. Techniques can be taught to employees to help them begin to think more creatively. Instilling creative skills in older employees and building a creative environment are likely two factors that can be achieved with limited effort on the part of management. This could result in an untapped resource of innovation. Organisations have to change from process based to purpose based, from analog mind-set to digital mindset,instead of hierarchical management structure – they should support peer to peer training and flat leadership models, instead of focus on individual talent management focus should be on whole workforce capabilities and performance, instead of perspective capabilities they need to develop adaptive capabilities, creating workforce as a place for experience and innovation

On the other hand, blue collar workers are now scarcer than white collar workers , growing blue-collar labour shortages result from educational trends, as people has attained more education, the group of working-age individuals with a bachelor's degree has grown, while the number of those without one has shrunk. Many blue-collar jobs have the potential to become automated in the next decade"

Employers believe that critical thinking and problem-solving will be the top two skills by 2025, writes Kate Whiting in an article for *World Economic Forum* (WEF), titled "These are the top 10 job skills of tomorrow – and how long it takes to learn them." *McKinsey Global Institute*'s (MGI) discussion paper, titled, "Skill Shift: Automation and the future of the work," sees a "substantial growth" in demand for technological skills – both basic and advanced. "Advanced technologies require people who understand how they work and can innovate, develop, and adapt them," the paper notes.

Digital skills are very much needed in the new age of automation, and according to the MGI paper, there is a "significant need" for everyone to develop basic digital skills. Companies will also look for workers with social and emotional skills – such as empathy and advanced communication. The discussion paper notes that the adoption of advanced technologies into the workplace will lead to an increase in the "need for workers with finely tuned social and emotional skills—skills that machines are a long way from mastering." Moreover, there will be a decline in the demand for basic cognitive skills, such as data processing or data input skills; on the other hand, the demand for higher cognitive skills, such as creativity critical thinking, decision making, and complex information processing, will grow through 2030, according to MGI paper.

We are usually apprehensive about starting over at middle-age. We spend our youth attaining skills that are supposed to help us achieve professional stability, job security, and success in our middle-age. So, the announcement that those skills are of no value could sound like a death knell. It can cause a physiological breakdown as well. But instead of being a bystander, watching technology take over human jobs and fretting about the future, middle-aged workers will have to swing into action. They have to proactively plan and adapt for the future.

Humans do not have the power to turn the clock back or can stop AI, robots, algorithms, and automation from becoming the most valuable employees of a company. But we are the most adaptive species, and we can use our brains to learn new survival skills. And there is just no age limit when it comes to learning new things. So, all is not lost for the middle-aged workforce in the new world of work.

During the Covid-19 pandemic, a large number of them rose to the occasion, thereby proving their capabilities and potential. They got accustomed to remote or virtual work in no time. They quickly learned how to work differently, how to leverage new technologies and collaborate with other virtual teams for better results. The middle-aged workers will have to tap into the same zeal to adapt and learn new things so that companies can continue to value them.

Many companies consider "older age a competitive disadvantage," writes Josh Bersin and Tomas Chamorro-Premuzic in an article titled, "The Case for Hiring Older Workers," published by *Harvard Business Review*. They note that older people are seen as "less capable, less able to adapt, or less willing to roll up [their] sleeves and do something new than [their] younger peers." Bersin and Chamorro-Premuzic believe that it is a misconception. They point out that scientific evidence has shown that even after they turn 80, people continue to increase their knowledge and expertise, which are the "two main predictors of job performance."

"There is also ample evidence to assume that traits like drive and curiosity are catalysts for new skill acquisition, even during late adulthood," according to Bersin and Chamorro-Premuzic. They also write that if the older people are "more intellectually engaged," they will contribute more to the labour market.

We might experience difficulties while learning a new thing at 30, 50, or 90, but this does not mean that our brain goes on a permanent strike. According to *BBC*'s article, "The amazing fertility of the older mind," our brain still has an "astonishing ability to learn and master many new skills, whatever [our] age."

Now, how do middle-aged workers convince the top management that they can perform the new tasks of tomorrow? A portfolio of new skills acquisition is the key to being part of the workforce in the new world of work. Middle-aged workers will have to look for platforms from where they can gain new capabilities. But, before that, they must do a serious evaluation of the skills that they possess as well as anticipate demands of the future of work. This will help them acquire skills that they need to perform new roles or transition to a new area of work. Leveraging online classes, webinars, and offline training sessions, middle-age workers can equip themselves with all the necessary skills needed to thrive in the new job landscape.

A company cannot operate without their experienced staff, and it is much easier to retrain and reskill them and make them perfect candidates for the new job than look for new talents. Hence, companies will have to invest in retraining and reskilling programs so that middle-aged employees can learn new skills to perform new jobs effectively. It will help increase productivity as well as ease the pain of transition for companies – ensuring that they continue to remain competitive in the new economic era as well.

Middle-aged workers cannot wait for a day more to start learning new skills. They have to step up now; otherwise, the future of work has no job for them.

Conclusion- Aging workforce challenges are something every company will have to deal with. There simply aren't enough younger workers to make up for the huge (skill) gap the baby boomers will leave behind. But rather than looking at the aging workforce as a problem, think of it as the great opportunity it actually presents. For all of the involved.

By working together with your employees, both young and old, you can find fitting, innovative solutions for every aging workforce issue. The use of technology and employee training, for instance, can be very helpful in this regard. And when you finally find the right solution, you'll see the tremendous added value that your aging workforce has for your entire organization

Anyone who stops learning is old, whether at twenty or eighty, anyone who keeps learning stays young-Henry Ford

Conclusion

The new world of work is getting built around machines and creativity. As a result of that, many jobs have disappeared, and many more will vanish soon. The adoption of automation, AI, robots, digital technology will enhance the productivity and competitiveness of companies, but it will also render millions of people jobless. Middle-aged workers are likely to be affected the most. They will have to upgrade their skills if they want to be considered valuable by their companies and enjoy the fruits of job security. So, without ifs and buts, middle-aged works should begin acquiring digital, social and emotional, technological, and higher cognitive skills. They are necessary to take advantage of the new opportunities in the future of work and not become obsolete.

****

Conclusion: Creativity in future of work

Future job landscape circa 2030: in a manufacturing unit, a robot is ordering a team of robots to speed up as there is a product-delivery deadline to meet, while another robot is managing the front desk and answering calls. And, AI-enabled computers are handling multiple tasks, including entering data, invoicing, completing financial statements, writing a press release, conducting experiments, engaging with customers, driving self-driving trucks and cars, and other routine work. It is not hyperbole or exaggeration in the least to state that AI technologies might become the undisputed overlords in the future of work.

Our workplaces, where we spend one-third of our adult lives, is poised for disruption. This dramatic change is going to upend more than a century old idea of employment and how we work as well as the established mode of business processes. And, it threatens to put millions of humans out of jobs.

It is not unusual to see the exit of the old-workforce and the influx of new ones, who bring with them a new set of ideas and new ways of doing things. But, this time influx will not be of another batch of the human workforce. It will be the robotic workforce that will march inside our factories and offices, across all industries around the world, taking over jobs and marking a good number of positions as "Only for Robots."

Initially, it will be the women who will disproportionately feel the brunt of the rapid automation and advancing AI technologies, as a large number of them are employed in low-skilled positions. These are repetitive and mundane jobs, and hence, the first to be automated in the upcoming years. As companies begin to adopt technologies in all industries and at all levels, we will see men, too, unceremoniously fired from their workplaces in the future. Soon, there will be a steady decline in the number of jobs available for humans, as advanced technologies will permanently occupy huge swathes of workspaces.

The technology trigged changes in our workplaces will also make lifetime employment dead. Gig work will be the new normal in the future of work; and the workforce will be made of freelancers, contractors, and consultants – the so-called gig workers. Companies will hire these workers for the short-term only. They will be asked to complete a specific task of a large project; therefore, only those will be contacted who have highly specialised skills and can deliver value to the company.

No field of work, sector, industry, or economy will be left untouched by advanced technologies. We can already see the impact of technology on the sales field. Instead of cold calling every individual in an area or bombarding everyone with a similar message, companies are now leveraging digital and AI technologies for prospecting. They are also using them to close a deal and convert potential customers into paying customers. And, as the role of frontline sales workforce is diminishing, we can see companies trimming it. Soon, there will be no place for them.

The rapidly advancing technologies are causing a seismic shift in job landscapes across the world. And there is no switch to turn off and stop this radical transformation. So, how do we handle this change and remain a valuable asset for organisations in the future of work?

Change is inevitable. It is all around us, and as Ancient Greek philosopher Heraclitus said in the 6th BCE, "The only constant in life is change." We cannot avoid it, neither in our lives nor in our workplaces. We will have to adapt to the new situation if we do not wish to fade away or become a wastrel. And, the adaption process starts with upgrading our survival skills, or in the case of our career, we need to begin by reskilling ourselves and learning everything anew. And, importantly, we have to know how to tap into creative thinking. Creativity is the skill of the future of work. It is the most innate human ability that no machine can replicate, and it will enable us to gain a foothold in the new job landscape.

Individuals with creative skills will be in great demand tomorrow. Companies will send talent scouts to even the remotest corner of the world to enlist the help of such individuals. It is because they will always require those who can dream up new solutions, solve complex issues as well as identify not-yet-noticed problems, and can make discoveries and invent an improved form of something. Creative individuals will enable them to remain competitive in tomorrow's innovation economy.

The burden of adaption is on companies as well, and not just employees. New technologies and trends are making many of them, who are not quick enough to perceive the new needs, go bankrupt. If they want to retain their competitiveness in the future, they have to find new ways of doing things, discover new market opportunities, and offer new solutions. For this, they will have to innovate; and if they fail to do that, they will perish and become history.

Leaders are required to foster creativity among teams and themselves, thereby designing their own future. Work-culture can only be improved by creative mindsets as they can re-think what things are and how they could be with their creative vision. Companies' need people who in today's scenario can bounce back from set-backs and can lead with flexible approach.It is one thing to be creative and other to maintain creative process. The business environment in which we are operating today,must have creative mindset in leadership for making creative workforce for turning challenges into opportunities.

Creativity is at the heart of innovation. So, a company will always need the help of humans to create its prosperous and fulfilling future. Innovation, however, never happens in isolation. Therefore, we will see collaboration between a diverse group of people -- most not located in the same country. This will enable the sharing of different ideas, the refining of ideas, and the exploration of varied possibilities for a better solution. Also, to provide each customer with an outstanding experience, companies will put in place a diverse and inclusive team. Members from different regions and nationalities, educational backgrounds, races, and expertise are more capable of inventing a solution that can be used by a majority of people across the world. And, when it comes to creative output, a diverse group will always overwhelm a homogenous group.

We cannot stop technologies from usurping our workplaces, but we can learn to work alongside them. We can learn how to use them as tools to make our work easier and amplify our capabilities. But, first, we need to reskill ourselves. We need to develop our creativity and expand our knowledge. It is our creativity that will empower us to become the dominant workforce in the future of work.

There will always be work for creative individuals. This may not be an end but new beginnings and there would be more layers which we need to add and cover in times to come.

Thank You

Reema Nakra